All Scripture references taken from the KJV of the Holy Bible, unless otherwise indicated.

Remember the Time

by Dr. Marlene Miles

Freshwater Press 2024

freshwaterpress9@gmail.com

ISBN: 978-1-963164-82-4

Paperback Version

Table of Contents

3

Remember the TIME

When Breaking Evil Covenants & Soul Ties

Freshwater Press, USA

What's Time Got to Do with It?

The peculiar thing about curses, hexes, and vexes, is how they transcend Time. It's as though they maneuver through Time and around Time and like a bad stain on an article of clothing, wash after wash, if a powerful stain remover is not applied, that mark will not come out. If Time is ignored in curses and evil covenants that curse never comes out. The purpose of this book is to admonish the reader to remember the time aspect of witchcraft, evil covenants, and curses and not to think that things will stop naturally on their own or that folks will get tired, or get saved, or get nice and suddenly leave you alone.

No, that is not a language they understand; you will not be left alone until you **make** them leave you alone. By that, I mean you must **make** wizards, witches and evil human agents leave you alone. You must **make** curses, demons, and devils leave you alone, and you must **make** evil covenants and the altars that they sponsor *leave you alone*.

Once an evil altar gets fired up, it stays fired up as long as someone is priesting over it. Witches die. Wizards die. Evil human agents die, but they often have already initiated some unsuspecting soul or some other willing evil person to take their place and carry on with their career of evil. In other words, no evil fired up against you, or your bloodline, will stop just because the person who carried the evil *spirit* or *spirits* died. The altar will keep going; it won't die until you kill it. You must **make** it die.

And it came to pass the same night, that the Lord said unto him, Take thy father's young bullock, even the second bullock of seven years old, and throw down the altar of Baal that thy

father hath, and cut down the grove that
is by it: (Judges 6:25)

Saints of God, when dealing with curses, and evil altars, especially if you are to tear them down or break them down, remember that Time is built into these evil covenants. Because of this, evil covenants transcend time. The devil is the creator of evil covenants, and don't you think he'd have some sneaky, hidden language in the covenant--, that, by the way, you may not even know that you're in a covenant, even if you were the one it originated with. Most likely, evil covenants that are attacking you are ancient and some ancestor somewhere in the world agreed to something stupid or demonic and put you and all in your bloodline on the hook with the devil.

However, **you** could be the lone reason there is an evil covenant in place that is affecting your life. **An evil soul tie is an evil covenant.**

A soul tie is a connection between two people that involves their souls, or in my opinion, the soul of one towards another, although the other may or may not be actively participating in it. Soul ties are described as being emotional, sexual and spiritual in origin. Fornication and immorality can form soul ties. In Genesis 34:2,3, Shechem's soul clave to Dinah. Solomon had the same problem, guess that's why he had so many wives and concubines. I picture Solomon, even in all his Wisdom, falling in love (lust) every day. A man (or woman) who wants everything they see is a weak person, they have an unprospered soul, they are immature and full of *lust* and *whoredoms*.

Deliverance is the children's bread. **Here, eat.**

A soul tie can be conducted by just one person because a person can be soul tied to an inanimate thing, or a non-human thing. A person can be soul tied to their dog and the dog loves them back. Another could be soul tied to their cat and if you think a cat cares about you, you are in your soul tie all alone. Soul ties are created through relationships—those that are successful **and** those that fail. They can also be created in the imagination of some who never had a relationship with the object of their soul tie.

An imagination gone wild is another reason why we are to cast down imaginations and every high thing that exalts itself against the knowledge of God.

A soul tie can be to a song. A person can be soul tied to a food and they may eat that same food everyday, and it doesn't even have to be *soul food*. It can be formed through relationships and interactions with certain individuals, such as family members, friends, co-workers, romantic partners, and as stated, even pets. Soul-tied families describe themselves as being close-knit. Yes, there should be a bond between family members, but a person's adversaries can be members of their own household, so don't deceive yourself. And conversely, be careful of inordinate affections.

Jacob's soul was tied to Benjamin which meant his life was wrapped up in his youngest boy (Genesis 44:30). Terah, Jacob's great-grandfather also was soul tied in Genesis. I can't prove this, but I suspect Judah was not letting Shelah go to raise up an heir to Er with Tamar because of a familial soul tie. After all his other two boys were dead for having attempted the same thing and he didn't want to lose Shelah also.

Blest be the tie that binds our hearts in Christian love (Colossians 2:2, 19). We expect to have love for one another in the church and in the faith. We don't always see that, but we expect it.

The phrase "soul ties" is not in the Bible but is a man-made description of human behavior. Soul ties are described as connections from one person's soul to (or into) another person's soul, as we see in BFF's, inseparable friends, super close twins, and lovers who love so deeply.

Well, at least, at the beginning of many relationships. But things can change. A soul tie can be between two people who are currently in a relationship, or between two people who *used to be* in a relationship, between two who are **not** now in a relationship, and sometimes between people who have *never* been in a relationship as in a secret admirer, someone who has a secret crush on another.

The object of the soul tie becomes an idol to the person who is soul-tied.

However, in relationships depending on how people function, one or both may bare their soul to another. An open soul makes that person very vulnerable because once a soul is open, all kinds of stuff can get in. Even children pray, *"I pray the Lord my soul to keep."* When the Word says to guard our hearts with all diligence, we can substitute the word, soul there. We pray for protection and restoration of our souls all the time, yet we may, in relationships, or in the *name* of a relationship lay open our souls for the object of our affections.

I recall a fellow often asking me *what was I thinking?* That was too much for me. He didn't need access to my mind, to my soul at that level. It wasn't that I didn't trust him *in general*, (at first) but because he kept asking me that, while not baring his own soul to me, I began to not trust him. When I don't trust you, I don't tell you anything. It's as though we've entered a warzone, and I will not be interrogated like a prisoner by someone I'm supposed to be in a relationship with. I suppose this is my rudimentary way of guarding or protecting my soul, which I am charged to possess in sanctification and honor. We cannot lay open our soul for everyone, especially by talking too much and telling too much of our personal business or even our secrets. This can be called ***discretion.***

While the Bible tells us to have a friend, we must show ourselves friendly, discretion is the better part of valor. Your children, for example, have no discretion as they tell everybody everything, with no filters, as if they must file a report of what goes on in your house to everyone they meet. We guard our words, we guard out hearts, and we also guard our souls.

It is said that when you have sex with a person you are basically giving *them carte blanche* access to your soul and at the same time believing that they will not kill you.

The devil and his evil *spirits* come not but to steal, kill, and destroy, so if you happen to be in love or in lust with, and have sex with someone who has demonic *spirits*, you are *risking* so much.

Even if you don't have sex with a person if you bare your soul to them, open up completely to them, they learn all your secrets, your weaknesses, and basically, your access points. If and when--, okay we'll be hopeful and say *if*--, if they turn on you and they are an ungodly, unsaved soul, you have risked everything although you never had sex with them. Such would be the case with fake friends, especially those that you used to think were BFF's.

The Bible says in Song of Solomon, *I found him whom my soul loveth* (Song3:4). When one has sex with another, their souls are open, it doesn't matter if they think they are just swiping right to do wrong—the soul is involved in sex. It is why the devil wants people to have illegal sex, so he can get into their lives very easily at that time.

Sex is an act of worship and where it is happening is an altar. Is it a Godly altar or an evil altar? You tell me.

Starting in Chapter 12, Abraham built an altar to the Lord and the account of that goes onto Chapter 25. Abraham split the animals and they were on the altar at dark and he had to run away the fowls that were trying to get or get at what was on the altar to God.

As soon as Abraham populated the altar with the chosen animals, and no coincidence, split them, that is, opened them up, here come the fowls of the air. In the same way on any altar, but especially an illegal altar, as soon as the altar is fired up, here come the enemies of your soul. No, you are a living sacrifice offering yourself to God, but at the same time offering yourself to your spouse, and each of you are vulnerable to one another. At that very time both your SOULS are wide open. You trust each other, and you should, but here come the foul *spirits* of the air.

Why?

They want in on this. If you have no spiritual guard or protection, this could be free for all. Recall in Song that Solomon set what seemed like a phalanx of guards at the door of his bedchamber. If that is a spiritual thing then we can believe the act, every time the act occurs it is as though *Kingdom Business* is being conducted and it is protected.

A Godly or an evil altar determines which "kingdom" the participants are doing "business" for. I repeat during the act of sex, your SOUL is open. It is open with the intent of being with your spouse, but depending on what the atmosphere is like and what is in there as to what *spirits* may be allowed in your bedroom.

Sex doesn't even have to be involved. "The soul of Jonathan was knit with the soul of David, and Jonathan loved him as his own soul, (1 Samuel 18:1). This is a way of expressing Jonathan's BFF connection to David and David's bond with Jonathan. If this is not a soul tie, it is very close   to   being   one.

We are warned against fornication in Scripture because we become one with whomever we have sex with. Sin with a prostitute, you receive the *spirits* they carry. Actually, they partake of the evil *spirits* you carry as well. During sex, evil *spirits* are transferred and exchanged.

The Holy Spirit is not transferred that way. Temple prostitutes are not of God and serve no godly purpose, at all. So having sex with someone to "purify" yourself or to receive some type of Godly spirit is not a real thing although some false religions promote that.

When illegal sex happens, evil *spirits* are transferred *at will*.

- Lord, forgive me for all sex I've had with wrong people, whether I was the victim or willing, in the Name of Yeshua.
- Lord, annul the transference of sexually transferred demons, devils and *spirits* from every wrong sexual encounter I've ever had – specifically those that did not involve a legal marriage partner, in the Name of Yeshua.
- Lord remove those 7 demons, and those 7 demons, and those 7 demons—all transferred demons from my soul that I may serve You, and prosper, in the Name of Yeshua.

> Do you not know that he who unites
> himself with a prostitute is one with
> her in body? For it is said, 'The two
> will become one flesh'
> (1 Corinthians 6:16)

The Bible does not speak of "fragmented" souls or "dividing" one's soul, but this writer believes that is a possibility for many reasons. Some of those reasons I found in the books, **Regions of Captivity** by Ana Mendez Ferrell, **Fragmented Souls** by Win Worley, and teachings on *Parts* by Daniel Duval, all with Biblical and deliverance ground support.

I Was That Person

Many people have wasted their own life while being in soul ties waiting, waiting, wishing, wanting and believing that So & So will come back to them, and that one day they will have a tearful reunion. This evil and incorrect idea is fed by soap operas, rom-coms, *familiar* and *lying*, and *deceiving, seducing spirits.*

Oh, and add to that list, in the natural--, pop music. Of course, you know who is running the pop music industry and culture; it is the evil marine kingdom, so why would you believe anything they have to say?

Yet, you *say* those songs, you play those songs, you sing those songs, you *pray* those songs, sometimes for years and years. All the while faith comes by hearing, so you are convincing yourself of one lie after the other. But hey, it's set to pretty music and everyone else is doing it. If you don't know who won a Grammy award this year, then are you even an interesting person these days?

I used to be that person. I used to have to know all the latest tunes and have them in my possession and be able to talk about my favorite artists as if I knew them or was related to them. Speaking of celebrities, my late father-in-law, Lord, rest his soul, used to say, *Is anyone coming to buy a replica of your work uniform to wear? Then why would you buy a sports jersey, pay all that money for it, and wear it? It is what those people work in."*

Good point, *huh*?

So, why is what someone else such as a celebrity is doing so important to us as if they are our relatives or in our intimate friend group? Mustn't we all consider that what they are saying and diligently compare it to the Word of God?

Careful--, the object of our extreme affections and ungodly desires can easily be promoted to idols in our lives. When we admire them so much to the point that we want an update on what they are doing every day, that smacks of idolatry. When we want to be like them, look like them, sound like them, shoot hoops like them, and even wear their work clothes, that is treading on idolatrous grounds.

God hates idolatry; He says it over and over in the Bible. Soul ties due to excessive, inordinate affection and unwillingness to let go what should be let go of is as the sin of idolatry. Evil soul ties must be broken even if you love them obsessively.

Lord, help us all to do as the Word says, not as the world says.

The Soundtrack

Well folks, if you take note of the secular music that you subject yourself to, you may find that it promotes a lot of your behavior, even the forming of soul ties. What you hear often and daily may become a form of "gospel" and you may end of doing as the singers sing instead of as the Word teaches, especially if you are not taking in any Word. Take inventory of the soundtrack of your life, you may become very aware that **the music you have listened to since you were young, has affected your choices and actions, even the way you *think*, all your life.**

Of note, even though rap is very popular right now, both Pop and R&B music of the 1980's and on is still very prevalent, still played and overplayed. Not only that, the 20-somethings of today know all of that music. Yes, they know the music and all the lyrics, and they also sing those songs over and again.

My theory–, and it's not a bad theory is that those songs and those lyrics worked; they really worked to pull down even God's people and lead them into wasted existences, bad decisions, and unrealistic lifestyles. So, if you're the evil marine kingdom, why not recycle those tunes and call them *classics* and continue to torment and diminish another generation and another ---? Music can be so insidious that folks don't even know that anything is happening to them, or that the music they listen to and sing had anything to do with what has happened to them, once something happens.

Are all the songs you like or love oldies? Then you might be living in the past. It doesn't mean don't listen to a favorite song ever again, but there you go. What are the lyrics of those songs that you love so much? What are they about? How do they make you feel? What do they make you feel like doing? Do they honor God? Do they honor anything good? What or who do they celebrate?

Those songs are your prayers. Especially if you don't pray, they are your *prayers*. If you do pray, those songs most likely **counter** what you pray.

> Out of the same mouth proceedeth blessing and cursing. My brethren, these things ought not so to be. (James 3:10)

Let's say you pray to God, perhaps every day, at least once. How many times a day do you say, sing, or play a favorite song – even one of doubt or unbelief? In terms of quantity, what's winning, the prayers of faith or prayers of unbelief? It may not be your fault, secular music is played in business establishments and many places you go. Not only do you have no control over it, you also may just sing along as if being *of* the world is okay when someone *else* is spinning the tunes. But the words, music, drumlines of that song are getting into you all over again just as when you were **in** the world. If there is a song that you are soul tied to, it is now reinforced. If it is a song that you used to be soul tied to, but you got saved and got over it, the devil just re-upped the evil covenant, whether you realize it or not. All this because you went shopping and lingered in a store or in the mall for some hours.

Let's say you know every word of the soundtrack songs of your life by heart and can sing them and do sing them without the song actually playing. Do you equally know or have any Psalms or songs of praise that you equally, or more than equally sing, praise or shout to the Lord?

Evaluate this to evaluate your prayer life. Then map out what you've been saying and singing and praying compared to what you've been getting in your life.

Is your *soundtrack* blessing or cursing you? Is it giving you false hope in your wilderness soul tie(s)? MJ wants us to **Remember the Time**. The lyrics induce us to remember the time we fell in love, when we first met, and when we first kissed. Lionel Richie is still singing **Hello**--, he has been for 40 years, and wondering if we are looking for him. Poor Adele is crooning **Hello** from the other side. My God of Mercy, what *other side*? It sounds like an abysmal chasm separated two folks and maybe only one of them wants to span the distance and get back together while the other is ignoring the woman. **That is the definition of a soul tie.**

Actually, all three of those songs seem to be about soul ties. Are any of these songs constructive to a soul that is soul tied? No. They tighten the ropes, chains and bonds.

If your life's soundtrack is blessing you, then most likely it will bless your foundation and also the lives of your children. If your soundtrack is cursing you, then it is cursing your children and your *children's* children.

Unless you are a passive one-celled organism--, which you are not, the soundtrack of your life colors your life and its outcomes tremendously. You are a complex being, created by God in His image and likeness, just a little lower than the angels. Therefore, in your position and authority, and over Time, you create your own soundtrack to your life. Do not let anyone else do it for you and most of all do not let the devil do it. All that music may sound good, but the lyrics. And all that beautiful or bumping music may drown out the real words that are what really build foundations, and lives, and speak continuously into your own future, and the future of your children and also *their* children.

A man can have what he says, but if out of your mouth flow blessings and cursing, which will prevail? It is why wise Daniel said, *I won't bow*. When the music is played, I won't bow to the image. Its why people are insulted when someone throws money at them and says, *Dance*. (Well, at least they should be insulted and refuse to do so.) This indicates that you are not a captive and not a slave to that person or that money.

Speaking to yourselves in psalms and hymns and spiritual songs, singing and making melody in your heart to the Lord;

Giving thanks always for all things unto God and the Father in the name of our Lord Jesus Christ;
(Ephesians 5:19-20)

Time In the Words

A witch or wizard brings power to their words by making deals with the devil, and for example, triangulating with celestial powers. A time twist is also incorporated into the words they enchant. By adding Time into what they are speaking some curses are automatically renewed, daily, monthly, and possibly forever, depending on how a curse, which is an evil prayer is worded. This time component is like a rope that wraps around the victim or intended victim to make them struggle endlessly. Helplessly on their own, they can't get out of the curse, alone. They cannot get out unless they call on a higher power.

That higher power is higher for many reasons. That higher power is the

Greatest Power and will never be defeated. All Power belongs to that Power. That power is higher according to our faith. Jehovah God is the Highest Power.

That wording is something they got from God: O Give Thanks to the Lord for His Mercy endures **forever**. According to our faith, it shall be unto us. Faith comes by hearing, so hearing the Word of God exclusively, or at least more than the words of the world will give us faith for what God says instead of us letting ourselves be programmed by what the world is singing.

Faith is a result of how much Word is in us and how much Spirit is in us because evil *spirits* will always try to counter faith, diminish faith and move a person into doubt and unbelief. And, he does it with a devilish, demonic power or anointing.

A person in unbelief may believe any old thing.

But the Power of God is the Greatest Power because it has power over everything, including Time. That Power is the Highest Power because of the Better Blood which is the greatest sacrifice. **Altars work by sacrifice--, Period.**

No matter what sacrifice was put on an evil altar, the sacrifice of Jesus Christ is always greater. HOWEVER, *you* tap into that sacrifice by faith; but faith without works is dead faith.

Therefore, by faith and because you have faith, you participate in that Sacrifice by offering two sacrifices of your own: One is yourself submitted to God as a living sacrifice, holy and acceptable, which is your reasonable service. Do this often, even daily taking up your own cross.

And he that taketh not his cross, and followeth after me, is not worthy of me. (Matthew 10:37-38)

To me, that means that if you get saved but don't think you have to change anything about yourself--, that you are good to go from Day One, you have deceived yourself. You have an entire flesh life and previous sin life to renounce and lay down, and that flesh of yours (and mine) must be crucified. It is too much to do all at once, so we give up something of this world and of this flesh life daily as we learn and grow spiritually.

The second sacrifice is a sacrifice of works that you offer up an acceptable offering that you **feel**–, you really feel it as a *sacrifice* when you put it on that altar. You cannot give a sacrifice that costs you nothing, else it is not a sacrifice. An oblation or sacrifice is when you give something that you would like to have or keep for yourself. A sacrifice is giving something that you love and think highly of. A sacrificial offering is giving something that has great value to you and you believe God, the King of kings will *receive* it.

Now that you've brought a proper sacrifice to God and placed it on the altar, start fanning the flames of Fire on that altar so that your sacrifices to God will have a sweet-smelling aroma to His nostrils. And, by your prayers, words, and faith-filled acts, fan away the foul *spirits* that are gathered to partake of something that is personal and intimate between you and your legal, covenanted spouse, and God. This is **Kingdom business**, and it has nothing to do with any demonic *spirit*, although evil *spirits* are trying to get in because both your **souls** are open because at that time that you are ministering to one another and also to the Lord.

Yes, we are still talking about altars and Abraham and sacrifices as we learn about the works that Abraham did, directed by God so that God would establish covenant with him. This is Kingdom Business, and the foul *spirits* of the air will ever try to get into it, unless you've set a guard, unless you've invited the Holy Spirit, unless you are protected from their interference.

Recall back in the Garden of Eden after Adam and Eve sinned that God got them out of that Garden, unless they live forever? Then does it not stand to reason that if the devil sneaks his way into a covenant with God that the devil can save his own *life* and live forever? And how may the devil be trying to accomplish that?

By getting into *forever*-**type covenants with men**. By trying to sneak into the movies without paying. By trying to get into the gala with no ticket--, it's all been tried before, but God is not mocked, the devil is not getting in or *back* in.

We cannot make covenants with the devil *for* God, or with God for the devil. **Once the devil is in a covenant, God is not. Once the devil is in a covenant, even if you are in it with the devil, it is deemed an evil covenant. God is not touching that. And if you want to stay in that covenant with the devil, God is not touching you.**

You're probably that way yourself. Once a person is friends with your enemy is that person still your friend? Allegiances and friendships must be considered when you are making connections and even doing business with folks.

I will be an enemy unto thine enemies,
and an adversary unto thine adversaries.
(Exodus 23:22B)

Choose ye this day, saints of God. Who will you serve? Who will you be in covenant with? Obviously, it cannot be both the devil and God, it cannot be darkness *and* Light. By man getting kicked out of the Garden of Eden, God has already told us what He's going to do with folks who have devil covenants. Then He says it all through the Bible.

The LORD God said, "Since the man has
become like one of us, knowing good and
evil, he must not reach out, take from the
tree of life, eat, and live forever."
(Genesis 3:22 CSB)

So, if you're caught up in a devil covenant in error or you need to get out of one, how do you do that? How do you get out of an evil covenant with a time component to it? A higher power that has authority over *Time* will stop the clock, not only while you untangle yourself from the entanglement, but that Higher Power will also help you get out of the entanglement.

Like getting out of one place to get to another, we have to get out of covenants with the devil in it to properly enter into covenants with God in it. If we change our minds and want to do devilish things, we void covenants with God automatically. We don't have both. Saints of God, we cannot have both. It is why we can't get saved and then run back into the world and still believe that God is okay with that; He is not.

How does that Higher Power get you out of devilish entanglements? By authority. That Higher Power has authority over everything, actually. **But you have to ask God, and submit to Him**.

Just as a policeman standing in the middle of a street holds up his hand and all the traffic will stop, this Higher Power can stop traffic. This Higher Power can stop planets, celestial bodies and Time. Because He made it. He made it all and everything God made obeys Him. (Except man, with his free-will wielding self. And then he's sorry later and still ends up calling on God.)

That at the name of Jesus every knee should bow, of things in heaven, and things in earth, and things under the earth;

And that every tongue should confess that Jesus Christ is Lord, to the glory of God the Father. (Philippians 2:10-11)

Because of Time being built into an evil covenant or a curse, whatever has happened to you may *still* be happening. It may renew ever so often or maybe the catastrophic nuclear fallout of it hasn't even happened yet. There are demonic time bombs, after all, and Remember the Time. We will find out later in this book that we must remember the **place** as well, but Time is invisible so we must be sure to remember that Time is part of covenants, even evil soul tie covenants.

Man & Time

Man knows little about Time, and this is especially evident in the way he lets Time run all over him. Time controls his time; Time controls his life because he has a physical body. Spirits are not subjected to Time in the same way that flesh is.

Time gets **put** into evil covenants, and that time component can confuse the average soul. We ask questions such as, *Why does this keep happening?* It's because **Time** is built into the covenant or the curse that is plaguing your life. For this reason it may keep replaying in your life, or even *throughout* your life and into your generations.

If you've ever played a video or other game with a timer on it, you can be so close to solving the puzzle, logically you can solve it, it is not too hard for you, but the timer goes off and you still may not win. You may feel that you can get out of the problem, but the timer either goes off, or somehow resets back to zero and you have to start all over again.

This explains rise and fall. This explains getting ahead, and then losing all ground you thought you had gained. The timer that you didn't even know existed went off and you had to go back to square one in a demonic game that is a curse in your life.

We need a higher power to get us out of this evil curse and covenant. We need a power higher and greater than the power that roped us into this evil covenant. We need Jesus.

Time is territorial; Time is regimented. Time is demanding, and unrelenting, unless it is commanded otherwise. Normally, Time waits for no man, but Time can be commanded. Time is repetitive and does the same thing over and over. That's its job, to be regular, consistent and mark seasons, years, days, months, hours, minutes and seconds. When the game is over what does the ref usually yell? TIME!

Time can be programmed to call a man back to a certain period, over and over. The evil covenant can call a person back to a place, a space, back to a time period because of Time being involved in the covenant, soul tie, or curse.

- Lord, let Time always work for me and not against me, in the Name of Jesus.
- Let all indicators of Time, the appearance of the sun, moon, and the stars be profitable to my daily living, in the Name of Jesus.
- Time, work for me. Time, work for me. Time, work for me, in the Name of Jesus.
- Lord, compress, enhance, expand, empower my prayers to go backward, forward, sideways,

upside down, circular, inside out and outside in—, anyway they need to go to catch me up, in my own prayers, decrees, and declarations to when witchcraft was being used against me and I did not know anything about it. Redeem the time so when witchcraft was being used against me, but i didn't believe it.

- Lord, redeem the time, in the Name of Jesus.

The One That Got Away

The soul tie, or the pain of a soul tie usually starts out with one thinking about *the one that got away*, or describing him or her to whomever has asked.

A fellow asked me if there was anyone in my past who made me feel like what's the use, why even bother to date or get married again?

Being a hopeless romantic, I told him, *No.* Believing in God and that there is a right someone for each and every one, I told him, *No.* Having seen people, Sarahs and Abrahams of all ages get married, and at all ages, I told him, *No.*

When someone is asking you about the one who got away, they are pretty much asking you if you have a soul tie, whether they know that's what they are asking or not.

But it's only a fantasy folks, you can only *imagine* how a relationship or a marriage would be with that person that you *didn't* marry. Even if you try to look into his or her current relationship or marriage it is not going to give a picture of what your life would be with that person. The way you two relate can only be determined by you two. While the external superficial stuff – how well off or how poor a person is, what house they live in may be on your radar, but that doesn't mean that if you were with that person that they would be well off--, you don't know. Their current spouse could be the cause of their being well off. Their spouse's family could have given them a financial head start in their marriage. Those two could be dwelling together in so much unity that God commanded the blessing over their marriage and lives. You don't

43

know. There is never a way to know how your life would be with them unless you took that path in life. Anything else is just wishing and guesswork.

Their current spouse could be the reason they are happy or look happy. There is no guarantee that if the two of you were together that either or both of you would be happy. You cannot appropriate other people's happiness for yourself, pick it up from their house and transplant it into your own.

You can't even know by what the person may tell you because everyone doesn't always tell the truth. Some tell the truth as they know it, as they see it. Others are flatly deceptive. Discern every *spirit*, folks.

A woman married a very wealthy man and he died. She then remarried to a man who pretended to be wealthy, but she found out he wasn't. A year into their relationship the new husband was trying to cheat, showing pictures of his wife's house and cars which the deceased first husband had left her. He was telling potential new dates that this was all his stuff. So, even if the women he was hitting on stopped what she was doing to get with that lying man, she would not see any of those things that he was showing off, since none of it was his or was ever going to be his.

My rule of thumb is, if you like what a married man has, or says he has, because he's obviously a liar and cheater, divide it by half or less, since when he divorces to get with you, he'll have to give at least ½ of it to her. If he has kids, that's up to 18 years of child support, and many Courts are making the man pay for college in these divorce decrees these days. So, whatever he looks like he has, if he divorces expect him to have about 30% of what you see him as having now.

Do you know how frustrated a *broke* or broken person can be? How do you think they'll treat you in their new but unfortunate state? Back in the day when both of you were young and carefree of course he treated you well. But you both have lived a little (or a lot) now and life has come at you both. Life has made you into the thing that your foundation dictated. It could be something that you may have known nothing about, but it has turned you into exactly what you would always be, absent Christ. The only way any of us can be different than or better than our family foundation is in Christ.

When people ask me about the college I went to, what will I tell them? Of course it was the best, I only went to one. I can't compare the experience to Berkley or Harvard or any place where I didn't attend college. The other colleges that I didn't go to are *the ones that got away.* If I didn't marry *the one that got away*, it is only escapism, it's only a fantasy to think how things might have been if I had married *that one.*

Go back into the past to try to solve a problem or a trauma, without Jesus, and most likely you will end up mentally repeating the problem and re-traumatizing yourself over and over again. Going back into the past won't put you two back together again. It won't change anything really. This is why we Christians have to be progressive and press toward the mark of the high calling and not wallow in the past with psychics and diviners. When someone is constantly talking to you about your past, they are a diviner and dealing with *familiar spirits* and second heaven demons.

The Lord says, **Behold, I will do a new thing.** Saints of God, be encouraged, God will not allow the old thing to be done away with unless He has a new thing for you. And, that new thing, the latter Glory shall be greater than the former. Always.

A Sword Between Two

Perhaps he isn't *the one who got away*. Even though you are thinking so highly and so much of him, perhaps he didn't get away from you. Perhaps God put a sword between the two of you. Maybe he was a blatant sinner and fell under judgment with God so God said, to that unrepentant sinner, **"You can't be with this one. This one is Mine."**

For your own protection, perhaps God separated the two of you. If you take some time and ask the Lord versus simply daydreaming about the past, you'd find out God's mind on this matter instead of just what you want or what you think. What you want may be completely soulish with no Scriptural bearing at all.

Now, once you find out if God has separated the two of you for destiny reasons, then you must respect that. If your destinies don't match and you two never should have been together, God may have called Time on the wasting of your time, or the wasting of your mate's time.

Perhaps one or both of you fell under judgment with God. It is by the Mercy of God that He would separate you from a person who is under His judgment.

Accept it. Move on, or at least move to where the Lord says for you to go.

Separations and breakups are not always because of rejection; perhaps God kicked them out of your connection or relationship.

Of course, be prayerful, we don't take everything lying down. A partner could of left due to witchcraft. More on that in my book: **Seducing Spirits:** *Idolatry & Whoredoms.*

Another Lust

Perhaps he was filled with *lust* or *whoredoms* and was drawn away by another lust. Better now than later before you two had been together for 15 years and had 3 kids together. Be thankful if God separates you from the unholy, ungodly, anti-destiny mate so you can move forward into your real destiny.

Yes, it hurts, and your spouse may be gone, but God my have said, **Good.** God doesn't tempt man, but if God allows a thing, He's using it.

As said, be prayerful, don't take everything passively, but if you have prayed and heard God and God did this, there is no need to be angry with the person who left the relationship or the connection. There is also no reason to be angry with the person who got with your person who got away.

The temptation was sent into their life, and they failed the test, and ended up leaving you.

Get over it. I hate to say that, but some things must be gotten over.

- Bind the *spirit of rejection*, all *anger, unforgiveness, hurt, bitterness, resentment, jealousy, and grief.* Whew! That's a lot to get over to get over a relationship.

If you don't, any of those *spirits* and many others gain a foothold into your life. And, by life, I really mean your very being--, I mean your soul.

Then said he, Lo, I come to do thy will, O God. He taketh away the first, that he may establish the second. (Hebrews 10:9)

The Soul Tie Must Break

A soul tie is an evil covenant, and it must break; it must be broken, or a man stays hobbled and crippled repeating days and weeks and years like the movie **Groundhog Day** or other time-warped, time-stuck movies that we look at and laugh at. But they are not funny and should not be laughed at, but learned from.

A man attempted to torment his wife throughout their 50+ years of marriage by throwing a former high school interest in his wife's face whenever he was feeling evil or lamenting that he married the wife of his youth. He'd say to her during verbal sparring bouts, *I wish I had married Carol.*

The wife didn't particularly care, at least after a while, and laughed when he made these dramatic proclamations.

After many years of marriage and having brought up Carol's name many times, even after the two had a lot of children together, there came a time that this former high school sweetheart came to visit this couple. Carol had been so exalted that anyone who knew about her would fear what might happen when that man saw Carol again and Carol saw that man.

One would wonder why the long-time wife would even entertain a visit from this *Carol*. What good would or could come of it?

The fateful day arrived, and so did Carol. What kind of woman would she be? Would she be stunning like a movie star? Would she be so rich that she'd arrive with a caravan or an entourage like the Queen of Shcba? Would she be a snob coming to finally collect *the one that got away* and break up this long-time married couple that had a whole bunch of kids together?

One car drove up; it was a late model, nice, clean—a luxury sedan; it shimmered almost like gold in the sunlight.

What? Carol didn't drive a Lamborghini or a Bentley? Nope, just a regular car.

Carol got out of the car--, she looked like a regular person. She didn't walk in slow motion as in a movie and her hair didn't blow in the wind. She also was not 30 years old; she was 60 or 70 years old.

What was the attraction?

The children of the couple looked at each other in disbelief. *This was Carol*? All these years, all these conversations, and ridiculous discussions over this woman--, *this* was Carol?

What is wrong with people? They fought all those years—*why*?

During the entire visit Carol didn't even notice the husband. That's because the high school friend, Carol came to visit the **wife** of that couple because she was the friend of the *wife*, and not the friend or the sweetheart of the husband as one would suppose from their conversations—I mean fights over the years.

That man was my dad, and that woman was my mother.

This was hysterical, but it wasn't the only thing that was hysterical: Carol looked so much like my mother that they could have been sisters or genetically close cousins, or even double cousins.

What?

Yup.

And, Carol came to visit the couple with her own husband. Dad was silenced. Carol was paying him no attention at all. He was not so much evil as he was soul tied. The couple had twins, and both had middle names Carroll and Carolyn, a nod to this woman. The man really was soul tied to Carol, and Carol had no clue. If she did, she probably would have Claire *Huxtabled* him and let him know a thing or two; Carol was feisty. My mom was respectful and appropriate, but she was no shrinking violet. My dad married the right woman--, somebody better tell him.

The Children

The long-time married couple had several children as before mentioned. One son got married but later divorced. During his marriage he and his wife had a child who was named after a girl he went to high school with; he obviously was also soul tied to a girl from high school.

Is this genetic?

Possibly, but many things are by nature, some by nuture.

One of the daughters of the couple got married and divorced---, but she couldn't get over the man that she had divorced. She appears to have been soul tied to him. Another daughter was married and then widowed--, do you think that daughter has any ability to get over that man who died so early in life? It appears that soul ties run in this family. If the father can't get over a lost love or lost opportunity, 40 years later, how is this being modeled for the children?

It's not. Well, at least not very well.

Even if it were, what is in the blood is in the blood. If it is in the family's foundation or if there is an ancestral or generational curse that this family will not process grief well or will not process loss, then it can be assigned to this family that their progress will be limited or non-existent because they will live in the past—in yesteryear.

If it gets in the blood, it gets in the family's foundation. Then, like termites—it has to be fumigated out of there, else this behavior becomes a family problem that goes into the generations. Does anyone else get tired of hearing, *Oh, that family is just like that?*

We should not all acquiesce to the negative things that we are born into, but endeavor to change and improve, be better, and get over hindrances and obstacles. We all can change and be different and be better--, in Christ. But we've got to be *all in* Christ, not just hanging out on the edge, or pretending.

My Soul Tie

For years I was soul tied to a fellow. I didn't think I was soul tied. I didn't even know what a soul tie was back then. But we dated for a while and communicated very well. He was very nice to me, of course, and we saw each other often. As humans can do, I got attached to him, and I felt that he was attached to me as well. I was certain that I loved him. I was also certain that he loved me, since he told me so, openly and more than once.

Oh, he was everything: he was saved, he was tall, he was smart, he was pretty much handsome, he was friendly, and he was my friend. He was amorous and attentive. He was *everything*. Perhaps he was too much; perhaps I idolized him, unawares, and God broke us up. Many years went by, and I thought of him often, if for no other reason than, I am my father's child.

Not in real time, but looking back at the story of Carol we can learn that my family doesn't get over people very quickly or very well. Secondly, since I considered him the hallmark, I compared every other guy I met or dated to him--, although neither he nor my new love interest ever knew that I did that, as we didn't stay in touch. Whether my family gets over people easily or not, we don't keep talking to those who move on to other relationships, or if we believe we have moved on, we leave the previous relationship, physically in the past. I may not have even known that I was comparing him to others, emotionally and in other ways, but I was.

I thought this guy was my soul mate when we were dating. I continued to think that even after we broke up. Trust me, he broke up with me decently, properly, and in person, he did not just ghost me. Then, because of the way my brain and heart were wired, he became my soul tie. I wasn't ready to break up with him yet --, I didn't believe that I'd ever be ready to break up with him. So, I perpetuated the soul tie for many years. Sadly, I didn't realize that I needed to break this soul tie after all he was the one who had said to me, *"I will always love you because once you love someone, you always love them."*

Since those years of my youth I have had to learn to get over folks, things, and definitely, soul ties.

When deliverance finally came regarding this soul tie and evil covenant – I woke up one morning and just **knew**. I wasn't soul tied to that fellow at all. I was soul tied to the **time period** of my life and that fellow just happened to be the person in my life at that time.

TIME. My soul tie was to a **time** period.

Holla Back

When a person is soul-tied to a place and time he or she may experience backward dreams. There is something there that is calling you back, or there is something there that you want or feel that you want. You either want to acquire that something or experience that something over and again.

That time period and location may be your happy place. It may be your happy time. It may be your happy meal. It may be the opposite of happy; it might be something that you'd like to go back and fix.

On a more spiritual note, it is said that when you have backward dreams and backward thoughts, wishing for the past that there is an evil covenant that is pulling you back there. Some demon or devil got worship there and you may have physically left that place, but the demon is declaring by calling you back that you owe it. What do you owe? Could be anything; it could be worship, it could be money or some other kind of sacrifice. Because these demons and devils are spiritual, they are trying to talk to your spirit, often while you are asleep and manipulating your dreams.

On a more positive note, the dreams could be from the Holy Spirit who is trying to tell you that there is a problem back there in that place, or as we remember the time--, there is a problem back in that time period. He may be trying to tell you to go back and fix that problem.

How do you fix it?

Spiritually fix it; you don't throw natural solutions at a spiritual problem. You must prayer-treat it. You are made in the image and likeness of God, therefore you are a spirit and God is Spirit. God speaks, so we do as God does: we _**speak**_. That is how you prayer treat, you speak. You cannot wish, hope, or _think_ the solution to a spiritual problem.

How do you get soul tied to a place? Where two or three are gathered in agreement and make covenant promises to one another a covenant is formed. If it is a soul tie it is an evil covenant because the devil is in it. If there is a demon, devil, idol or little-g _god_ that believes it is doing something for you and you partake of what it thinks it is doing for you, like a freelance demon, it now believes you owe it. I say _freelance_ because you didn't **ask** for a demon to come and help you do anything, did you? No, the demon just showed up simply because what you were doing or were about to do was a sin and it has auspices to show up where sin is going on.

If Time is involved in what it believes you owe it, then as far as it is concerned, you must **keep repeating** the act regularly or at certain time intervals or you are in breach of a contract that you didn't even know existed.

I say you, but these evil contracts and covenants could be coming through your ancestral bloodline created by some old dude or old lady that you never met who could have been dead for hundreds of years. If time is built in, which is why I admonish you to Remember the Time, these evil covenants don't expire. Like BaeBae's kids, they don't die, they multiply. You must kill it! **Make** it expire!

Unless we are talking about a soul tie that formed in your own life time with you and someone or something. You can't blame an ancestor for that; that is your own doing.

Again, why are we being called backward?

Where did this particular memorable act take place? That is where the altar is. Where was the evil covenant formed? That is the place of the altar. Where were you when this relationship formed, happened, or either broke up? That is where the altar is. If the altar is calling you back, the place is where the altar is.

The proclivity to form soul ties may be seen as a pattern in families, but soul ties are not inherited or transferred generationally.

Person to Person

What things tie people together? Pain. Joy. Pleasure. . Need, and other kinds of *bonding.* Person to person, people get together by forming pain cliques and may get soul tied that way.

How did I get soul tied like that? In my eyes and in my estimation my life was going the way I wanted it to at that time. I was young, fit, could lose weight in 3 days, happy, nothing hurt, had finished school, had just started my career and was finally getting paid after years of student-induced sacrifices. Here comes this guy, like-minded, with similar interests and a similar career. Oh, we'd make such a good couple, I had probably silently decided in my mind. And the fact that he came around so often confirmed that he must be thinking the same.

Did he ever say that?

Yes. Plenty of times.

Not only that, this was the right *time* in both of our lives that I should be thinking about marriage and starting a family. This was the guy; my twenty-something year old mind confirmed it, deep into my soul.

I'd be patient. This is the one, and our connection felt so strong and so right that even if he goes away or starts dating someone else, he's coming back to me. That is at least what my favorite R&B song said. It was confirmed in the musical **soundtrack of my life**, so it must be true.

I liked myself then. Life hadn't hurt so much *yet*. I didn't even expect that life would ever hurt. There weren't that many disappointments—yet. There was still hope. His mom had even declared over us that he and I had a bright future. His dad approved of me and us as a couple, therefore, hope was alive so that meant that faith was working in my life. Faith the substance of things hoped for, the evidence of things unseen.

The bright future was still ahead of us and if we are turned in the right direction, we can see it or at least see glimpses and glimmers of it.

Later in life people may wonder if there is a bright future, and if it is, why can't we see it? Are we facing in the right direction still? Why is it taking so long.

Did we miss it?

Did we blink?

Did we sleep through it altogether?

Or, did life call us, calling us forward, or is life trying to pull us backward? Are we stuck in a soul tie, looking backward instead of on our bright horizon and the promises of God?

Lord, help.

The Good Old Days

Folks, consider your good old days soberly. Being soul tied to teen years is why Al Bundy and so many others yearn for high school or college days again. Those were very good days. It was fun and most of us had no bills and little obligations during that phase of our lives. Most of us were free, we had no kids yet – not that we disparage kids, but they are non-stop, and they are a lot of work and expense. Days of freedom can be very enticing.

So, you may start to think about the past, or the past may be coming to confront you—making you think about it. Someone from the past suddenly calls, you see them at the mall, or they show up at your job or house. But when reflecting, when building your memory--, your fantasy you pick the best period of your life. Next, you've got to insert in some people, and *who* gets inserted there? The most fun, or best-looking person, or if you are really in pain, either the person who caused the most pain during that time, or the person who you feel loved you the most through the pain you may have endured.

It's your fantasy. It's your memory--, you must be the star of this little blue sky drama.

How many times will you imagine this? It depends. It depends on how hard your current life is. It depends on how much GOD you have on board. It depends on if you live in reality, or if you are prone to *escapism*. It depends on if your needs are being met emotionally at this time, or if you feel that they are.

Are you one to live in the day, or do you forever wish for yesterday? Do you live in the now, or does something draw you back often?

The man who adored *Carol* was my dad. Often my dad would speak of the past, and as often my mother would ask him why he spoke of the past all the time? Dad couldn't hear what she was saying because the past must have been in dad's **blood**. That was commonplace to him to think like that. *His* dad may have thought that way, so Dad probably didn't see anything wrong with it. Upon closer inspection I noticed that the past also had vestiges or tenacles in his children's blood--, some more than others.

Dad's children also had the tendency to dwell in the past. I may be writing objectively here, but I am one of my dad's children and I had to take a look at myself and my reminiscing tendencies, as well.

Being always or often pulled backward is a curse. Curses are in place because of evil covenants. Evil covenants are not of God. Curses in family foundations are passed on to the children of that bloodline. This must be dealt with spiritually; else it remains or worsens. In the bloodline or in the foundation, Time must be considered here because what's in there is really in there. If it's in the foundation, it's pretty much a copy and paste for every child that is born of that bloodline. The kids could look different, some taller, some shorter--, physical characteristics may vary, but the foundation has been copied and pasted into each child.

The only way out of fulfilling the mandates of a foundation is to be in Christ Jesus and to be fully in. Further, one will have to renounce and denounce family and ancestral sins, curses, evil covenants and all things evil that repeat out of that foundation.

Thinking and talking about the past seems harmless --, why would a couple fight over this? Because it is not harmless, and they will continue to fight if things are not addressed *spiritually*.

As mentioned earlier, a person can be soul tied to another or other family members. A family, or at least the dad or the decision maker of the family was soul tied to his own college-bound kid, so the family picked up and moved to the state where the child wanted to go to college. This included the closing down of an entire medical practice. I've moved my dental practice before, and it takes a good solid year to do that correctly. It's not easy. The credentialing part takes the longest. I can only imagine what is involved in moving a medical practice to another state.

Another woman always said that when her child went to college she would move on campus with the child. She had no qualms about letting it be known that this was her favorite child and she wanted to be wherever that child was. Her child is now 40+ years old and the two of them are still together. Soul tied. Actually, the mother is more soul tied to the child than the child is to the mother. The child is an opportunist.

A person can be so into another that one is taking advantage, but the victim seems soul tied and won't leave the aggressor alone.

If your last relationship messed up your mind because you refused to let the relationship go--, let it go now and be restored, in the Name of Jesus. Lord, restore my soul and let this mind be in me that was also in Christ Jesus. Sometimes you cannot let the relationship go, for example, if it is your child or your parent, but you must re-order and re-structure the relationship by Godly parameters and set proper boundaries.

College seems to be as harder or harder than a child going to kindergarten for some parents. Another mother could not walk by her child's room after he went to college without crying for the first year. Lord have Mercy--, the boy didn't die, he went to college.

Another mother turned into an ogre when her only child, a son went to college, We'd been knowing her for more than 10 years and we did not recognize her his entire Freshman year in college. (You know I told her, *right*? Somebody had to tell her. I simply asked her why was she upset that her child went to college? She had no answer.

Then I asked her did he say he had met someone and was bringing a girlfriend home to meet the family?

She said, *No.*

Then she settled down a bit; at least there was no female to "replace her"--, yet. I believe this may have been the beginning of the return of her emotional sobriety.

When her college kid came home for summer break, he got on her nerves, and she got over him. Now, she's nice and normal again. The boy wasn't soul tied to her, and that may have been her problem. Maybe she wanted him to call her every night crying that he wasn't stuck up under his mother anymore. He didn't and now that the soul tie is broken; she is herself again.

Separation is hard and often it is nearly impossible if there is a soul tie involved. Can you see how each of those women basically **wasted** an entire year of their own lives because their child went to college?

The *waster spirit* is a *spirit* from hell. It is real and its job is to make people waste time, relationships, money, and ministry opportunities, among other things.

You can see how being soul-tied is a losing proposition and wastes time and life, yes?

Sending Forget-Me-Nots

Territorial powers, and other *spirits* bring remembrances of times gone by... to pull you back into that time. Demonically charged memories are designed to pull you backward. Pray to the Lord that you remember things correctly, truthfully, and as they were, not as you wanted them to be, in the Name of Jesus.

The spirit of grief, the spirit of pining away, and the spirit of backwardness are all dangerous and *waster spirits.* All these spirits either make a person get stuck in a place like miry clay or quicksand so that they can't free themselves. Or if they do manage to get away they get sucked back into that vortex. A person could get a few steps away or very far away but if Time is built into the curse that draws a person backward, and if they don't have Christ, and therefore no defenses up, these forces may have their way and drag a person back kicking and screaming. Or, if they are deceived, they may willingly run back into their past, thinking that they are doing a good thing, or they are going back to the neighborhood to show how successful they've become now.

It's a trap, folks. As soon as you put yourself back in the place of that altar and start doing the stuff you used to do, you will renew the evil covenant, giving it a stronger foothold than before, unless you go **_in Christ_**, and seriously prayed up. Sometimes you must go back and you should go home and to reunions if you desire, but go **prayed up.**

Your favorite song from yesteryear can pull you back. It can put you at the football game or in the movie theatre or wherever you were when you had your first kiss or some first memory that you probably shouldn't have. I say that because evil soul ties have the devil involved, so therefore sin was probably involved in the creation of the soul tie that is leading to the backward event.

Your favorite place is now a memory that you think of often. You are thinking of it because it is drawing on your spirit and soul.

Your favorite restaurant or food where you used to go--, where you used to meet your friends. These are all possible soul ties or soul-tie triggers. And yes, if you are prone to soul ties, you can have more than one soul tie. Some people are very emotional and nostalgic, and their entire life is lived in memories. Facebook sure finds memories for us. My cell phone finds memories that they do not need to find. For this reason, we should purge our accounts and devices when we must move forward. *Just saying.*

All those things *call you back* and call you backward all day and all night if your spirit man is not built up to resist. All these are tugs on your emotions which is part of your soul. If you are soul-led, and especially emotion-led, or flesh led you will be enticed to experience the same stuff all over again like Blues Clues.

Like cookies on your computer, sites you've visited will have pop up ads all over your screen while you are trying to do something important. Whoever or whatever you were *serving* back in the day will keep sending you pop up ads, pop up memories come to draw you back to the good ole days. There you may have a pleasant memory, or maybe a frustration, but something draws you back either in a memory, or in a dream.

In a dream you may get stuck there having the same dream repetitively and not resolving whatever needs to be resolved. What you *shoulda* said, what you *shoulda* done, what you could have done differently to get the outcome you think you really wanted at that time, but did not may still trouble you. If you don't rust that that what you did may have been the exact right thing, and the two of you should have been separated after all you may be plagued by frustration.

Nudges, reminders, and forget-me-nots are all signs that *the past* **wants you back**. That is Time working to keep you from progressing. But that memory can also work to draw you back to a place and space. So the dimensions of space and time can work together to draw you, pull you back and sometimes backward.

I can't get over so and so.

Really?

I keep thinking about them.

Yeah, but that ship has sailed, and they've already moved on and married such and such. And, did you know a familiar spirit can do that and make you think that it is you who is thinking about that person? In the world they say if you are thinking of a person that person is thinking about you, but that is a LIE. It is a set up and another trick; God doesn't deal in telepathy, but if you think that mutual thinking of each other is a thing, then you are trading in psychic, ESP and telepathic energies.

But what if I could see them one more time, to get closure?

Saints of God, if it's been 10 or twenty years and you haven't closed a matter yet, then you are the problem. When you can't tell if something is closed or not, better ask God. A thing could be closed already, but you are the one who doesn't want it closed, or you may be under the spell of a *familiar spirit* to make you want to leave something that is closed, open. This may cause you to be pining away wishing for yesterday or yesteryear all over again, wasting time, wasting energy, wasting money. Wasting life.

Bind up that *spirit of dissatisfaction,* in the Name of Jesus.

In the same way, the *spirit of grief* puts a permanently lost person that you may have been soul tied to on your mind all day and night if possible. The deceased person is not thinking about you; they have no memory of this life. That *spirit* is not trying to pull you backward, it is trying to pull you into death and hell. Do not be deceived.

- I bind the *spirits of grief, excessive grief, death, hell* and the *grave,* in the Name of Jesus.

Remember the TIME

So, when breaking soul ties, remember to break the *Time* factor out of the evil covenant that stands against you, or the soul tie may linger.

What time factor?

If you had anything to do with the soul tie and most likely you do, you may have told the person that you can't get over, or can't seem to function without that you would love them forever, or to infinity, or whatever cute thing you said. YOU introduced **Time** into this declaration and basically put a clock on the evil covenant. With soul ties, no witch or wizard did this to you; you did this to yourself, with your own words. Granted, they were probably childish, immature, passion-filled, puppy-love words, but you did it yourself. Therefore, with the help of God, you need to renounce these words and fix this, yourself.

Like the lyrics from too many love songs that may be on the soundtrack of your life: You'd love them *forever* and *always*. You'd wait for them *forever*. You'd marry them *a thousand times*. You'll love them more every day. You want to grow old with them. Every sunrise, every time the moon or the stars appear. Every time the waves of the ocean wash in, as the seasons change--, there is no end to how many ways you or whomever spoke the vow put **Time** into the equation of your soul tie, which has now become as a curse to you.

This means that you would not be able to function as a separate human being if you did not have this person in your life—if they left, if they died, it basically was a vow, and now you look either like a liar, or you must fulfill the vow. The person may have made no such vow for you, and you may be wondering why don't they love you like you love them? They may love you, but they didn't make an excessive, over the top vow that basically became a curse to themselves. For this reason, I believe that one person is in the soul tie and the other has gone on with their life. It doesn't have to be both parties are soul tied to each other, like Romeo and Juliet, although the demonic *spirit* present in the soul tie may have you thinking that. And that is one of the things that makes you continue to hope and wait for this person to return to you.

When you were in the act of making a covenant with this person, whether you knew you were making covenant or not – you may have hoped you were tying the two of you together, *forever*. But while in this process, while your soul was open, you went in and took out a part of your soul and either wrapped it around that person or that person's soul or presented it to them saying, *Here I am, take thus and so part of me and do with it what you will*. In so doing did you hope that they would say, *"Oh wow, she* *really loves me so much, this should seal the deal because I was looking for the person who would love me the most that would do whatever I said and that I could **control**."*

That is not love, folks--, that is one of you submitting yourself to be the other person's slave.

Anyway, you made a vow by saying, probably silently, that you were willing to bet your soul or lay down part of your soul on the altar of what you may have thought was Love, to ensure that this covenant forms, is accepted, ratified, and lasts. Time is in it now—that it lasts, and lasts forever or to infinity, or to eternity or some hyperbolic time frame.

Even a covenant marriage is until death do you two part; Time is in a legal Godly marriage as well.

There is a woman who declares she wishes her children would stay babies. Since that is impossible don't do that; remember the Time. Do not make vows that include **Time** because as they say, Time marches on. Things progress, they must if they are alive. Do not wish that your child would not grow up. There are many horrible ways that can be made into a true statement. You do not want any of those things to happen to your child or your family.

Your mouth is powerful; be ever so wise in what you say.

- Lord, let my mouth speak Wisdom and let the meditation of my heart be filled with Understanding, in the Name of Jesus.

You Must Break Soul Ties

You must break evil soul ties
because:
1. They diminish your life.
2. The devil is in them.
3. They inhibit soul growth and prosperity.
4. You are not a whole soul with one or more evil soul ties.
5. You are not really tied to the person that you believe you are daydreaming about and yearning for. You are tied to a demon who is impersonating the person you long for.
6. You are captured and in captivity.
7. They limit you spiritually, emotionally, mentally.

8. They make you cruel to others. You may feel that you don't need other people, you feel more like you need the person you lost or are pining over. So you may disdain others, or miss other divine connections that will move your life forward.

9. Soul ties are a waste of time and they make you waste time and lose time.

The severely grief-stricken may stay home to "talk to" or grieve over their lost relationship rather than be out and about with the living

10. They make the person you are tied to into an idol. Whether you love them or hate them, if you think about them more than God or more passionately --, good or bad, they have become an idol to you.

11. They keep you from moving forward. Terah couldn't move past Ur because he lost a son there and he was buried there, (Genesis).

12. They stagnate you. You are going nowhere. If your soul is in the past

and your body is in the present, where is your future? Your body doesn't go any place without your skin, then how do you think you can go forward leaving your soul behind?

13. Soul ties cage you in that relationship, but really they cage you in that time period.
14. They arrest development.
15. They block your blessings from God.

Yes, the trauma of losing that person could be dramatic and traumatic. *How* you lost the person is as important is that you lost.

A flood, a fire, an earthquake, and any other sudden destruction may come upon a person; Lord forbid. But, those traumas may cause you to change and be different, so much so that the person you are with at that time can't deal with you and they may fade from your life or step away completely and suddenly.

The brain is powerful and curious. Logically, we may think that something on the **outside** of us is why the loss of a relationship happened and we may try to recreate the scenario where we were living in to bring that person back. When it is not the external stuff that kept the person there--, well, it shouldn't have been, but there are those types, too.

It was, or should have been the internal you, your internal joy and happiness, your peace, your shalom – the Fruit of the Spirit that was exhibited in you that attracted people and kept them around you at that time.

You liked yourself.

You were well connected to God and so the Holy Spirit was able to shine through you. There was Fruit of the Spirit coming forth in your life; that is how anyone is able to stand anyone else. But when something happened, you changed, and you became harder to be around or harder to get along with. The change *back* now needs to be you, not your environment, not others, not a new spouse or a makeover surgery, not anything external. No, not a new car or a new outfit or a new look.

You need Jesus and you need to put Him on fully. The change needs to be internal and spiritual.

One Way, Two Way

Soul ties are described as a two-way connection, while a one-way soul tie is called an obsession.

The bond shared between two people who are connected by soul ties can be strong and long-lasting. Unfortunately, not all soul ties are positive ones; some cause us to become attached to unhealthy relationships. Other soul ties may be residual after a relationship is over--, if the relationship ever existed at all.

The following are signs that you may be in an evil soul tie.

- Feeling anxious when away from the other person for too long

Men sometimes think that women are clinging vines. Some may be, but in truth, the helpless, needy woman that a lot of men think is adorable may be the one that is easily soul tied and needs to know where he is every moment of the day and night. She's not trying to accuse you of anything man, she's weak and needy and soul tied. You thought that is what you wanted in a relationship, but are you seeing something different now?

I say that in the authority that I've heard more than one man tell me that I didn't need him, and that I was too strong. Folks, I'm sweet as cherry pie, but I know who I am in Christ. So, these fellows went on to find delicate and helpless types – oh well. I thought being a whole soul and knowing who I am in Christ was not only attractive, but it was what was expected to enter into a relationship with others in any capacity.

Further signs of being soul tied are:

- Being dependent on another for emotional support.
- Can't make a decision without the input of your soul tie.

People please--, it's as though your spouse or mate has the other part of your brain. They don't. Well, they shouldn't.

Emotional support animal--, emotional support *person*. Why are your own emotions not enough to manage the things in your life that need to be managed? What happened to your emotions? Are they tied to another? When you are soul tied, your emotions are on lock down, in captivity and are essentially not available to you. They are occupied with thoughts of your lost love.

If you are away from the presence of God and you feel lost, hurt, empty, that's one thing, but if you are away from a person or a thing or whatever you have soul-tied yourself to, you should not have that level of anxiety.

Folks, this exalts another person to an idol if you can't function properly without them. Can you see this?

- Struggling for your identity without them.

I've noticed some avatar or banner pix online are the man and the woman together on her page, yet on *his* page, it is just a picture of him without her. Sometimes he may not even mention her or that he is in a relationship. Is this a soul tie or a *hot mess*? Or, is it both?

- Feeling stuck. Being stuck.

Don't convince yourself that being soul tied means you love them, the most. Don't convince yourself that it is okay; it is not. Do not buy into the twin flame rhetoric, it is demonic and is not true; God does not split souls and put one half a soul in one person and the other half in another person and then challenge them like it's a survivor race to find each other. Okay, let me say God doesn't make a soul and then the mirror image or exact replica of a soul and then put one in each of two people and then dare them to find each other so they can function together.

First of all, God has enough souls to go around for each person. And, this sounds like some demonic devil experiment—splitting souls, because the devil has no souls and he wants to take one and spread it out? This is ludicrous.

And, God wants you to make divine connections and meet up with your destiny helpers and intended spouse. It is the devil that wants to keep the two that God wants together, apart.

Soul Tied to a TIME

A person can be soul tied to the good times, to the better times in their life. A time period when life was way different than it is now. Chronically wishing for the past can lead to bitterness and dissatisfaction. The time when your house **wasn't** flooded. The time when your house **wasn't** on fire, and you stood there helplessly and watched it burn down. The Time when Grandma was here. You can be soul tied to a person, a place, a thing, and I add now – a Time, an era, an age--, a time period.

I am challenging you in this volume because this happened to me. I wasn't really soul-tied to a person, but I thought I was. I was soul-tied to a time period. That was error enough, but within the error, I erred thinking for years that I was soul tied to a person. Thank God that He didn't hear and answer my soulish prayers to get back with a perceived soul tie; surely that would have been a disaster.

Still, we can be soul tied to people, but we must rightly divide truth from wishes and from lies to evaluate where we are in life so we will know how to prayer-treat it and how to get out of the problem situation.

Territorial powers can also call you backward to a place. The way to prayer treat that is to declare that you are in Christ, all in, and that you are no longer subject to any territorial powers of your past or any place that you've been to, stayed at, lived in, or traveled through, in the Name of Jesus.

Copycat City

The devil copies things, and then perverts those things. If you can imagine what God has for you, the devil will have something *like it*. Your soul tie may be *like* your real kingdom mate. God didn't allow that previous relationship because either it wasn't real, or it wasn't time. It could have been a demonic deep-fake.

You did pray about this connection, *didn't you*? You didn't? Then, no wonder. If you are not praying, anything goes--, that is anything the devil inserts into your life may come into your life and stay there.

My dad was emotionally soul tied to *Carol*, so I'm not surprised that I latched onto a nice guy and held out hope for years, calling it faith, hoping that we would get back together. Sad, really. I wasted more time than the women who suffered when their children went to college.

If you think of the numbers of people and the amount of time they waste waiting for Mr. Right to return, when if he didn't think you were Ms. Right, then he moved on to become someone else's Mr. Right. That guy that I thought was my soul tie didn't get married for a long time, so the idea that a grand reunion was in the plans, was an effective deception that the enemy used to keep me off my right marital timeline. No man knows the day or the hour of the Lord's return, but we are not waiting for Jesus--, it's a man. Plus, good girls are not supposed to be in the streets trying to meet the next fellow; they should stay home and **wait**.

Oh, I fell for it. Perhaps because I wanted to. I had plenty of suitors, that I *didn't* want to marry. I probably only went out with guys that I would never want to marry, because I was waiting for the special one.

Don't let that be you; don't waste time. Don't waste your marrying years.

Lest thou give thine honour unto others,
and thy years unto the cruel:
(Proverbs 5:9)

Eventually, my heartthrob got married. He came to see me when he was planning to marry. I told him, *Don't marry her,* but he did it anyway. A few years later, they divorced and hope in me surged. We were both single again at the same time. We saw each other, went to church together, prayed together, discussed the Bible and stayed pure together--, this time. Oh, this had to be the grand reunion.

It wasn't--, he married again--, to someone else other than me. Again.

Oh, it was worse than that. I met her and he *used* me to make her jealous, and then he married her.

Had I not been soul tied, or believed that I was soul tied, I never would have fallen for that foolishness. So, I can add:

16. Soul ties make you stupid.

Grape Jelly

Soul ties are evil covenants that get embedded in your foundation and will keep bringing you the *same-ole-same-ole* over and again.

Next thing you know your kids are doing the same things you are doing. Your children are not involved in your soul ties, but the proclivity to linger too long in the past or not be progressive enough may get *copied and pasted* onto your children. Evil covenants get implanted into a foundation; not the covenant of the soul tie, but the covenant of maybe this family doesn't move forward quickly from relationships, or this family wastes time, this family is so nice that they fall for almost anything, or this family loves too deeply or incorrectly--

, possibly bordering on idolatry. The soul tie is the expression of those possible foundational covenants, and those traits indicate what *spirits* are embedded in that foundation.

If you spill grape jelly on your kitchen table and never wipe it off, it hardens and then it gets stuck there doesn't it.

Forever?

Seems like it. It sure takes a lot of muscle to get it off and my goodness, don't damage the table while you are cleaning up this mess that could have just been wiped off easily the moment or even the day it happened, but it's been weeks and months, and years and it is still there. Stuck.

Some people are so stuck they are living in the last century while the rest of us are in this one. Some are still in the last decade while time has moved on.

They may have been so shocked or so traumatized by the break up, divorce, loss, or change, that they haven't found a place to file that information in their mind, in their brain, in their soul. There is ample capacity for that in their spirit, but if their spirit man is not built up, or they have not tried to access their spirit for help that *stuckness* is like the glob of grape jelly perched on a kitchen table.

Some live emotional and soulish lives--, it's all they know. The person who lives by the soul, mostly emotions, is most likely the type to be soul tied. They not only live by their soul, they lead by their soul. Their soul directs them. They go by what they *feel* like, by moods, and by what they want and wish to happen.

Something started out very sweet, like grape jelly. But now Time has gone by. An evil covenant has had a chance to be created, harden, and incorporate itself into the table of your foundation. It's done it's damage before you try to scrape it off. It has affected the finish on the table, the gloss, the glow, the shine, the glory. It's disgusting to see a glob of jelly stuck to a beautiful wood table.

And, even worse, it is heart-wrenching to see evil *spirits* that should not be there, present and implanted into a family's foundation--, hardened there, determined to stay to wreck and ruin that family and its bloodline.

Saints of God, we have so much work to do to get this cleaned up.

Don't Snooze

Don't snooze, but if you do, don't snooze too long. How many of us have hit that snooze button and gone back to sleep fully and missed our correct wake up time, been late for work and missed the meeting or the connection entirely?

Saints, you don't know what else you missed that day. There could have been a divine connection for you on the metro, or on the subway, at the coffee shop that you usually stop at. There could have been a divine connection at the bus stop that would have changed your life. Yeah, I'm talking to you, you could be someone who really needs their life changed. But a backward pull, a frustrating dream, a fight with your emotions, and you then escaping by daydreaming about *the one that got away* sabotaged your day.

God could have orchestrated blessings for you today – every morning, tender mercies. Daily He loads us with benefits. But if you were feeling blah, or the soul tie or the blues had tied you to the couch or to the bed, you could have snoozed a divine opportunity sent by God. After all, if your soul is in 2005 but your body is in 2025 how can you possibly leave home if you don't have yourself *together*? And, I mean that literally.

Have you ever stopped to think what blessings and opportunities may have gotten away from you while you were distracted thinking about *the one that got away?* It's like fishing--, how long will you think of that citation bass that you didn't catch while the pond is full of even bigger fish that you can and *should* catch?

What if 20 more chances, opportunities, or *fish* got away while you are looking backward thinking about the lowly *one that broke up with you, got off the hook and swam away?*

If your bright future is ahead of you, how will you ever see it? How will you ever catch the vision of how wonderful God has prepared your life to be if you are facing **backward**?

A soul-led life, versus a spirit-led life, is easy to bewitch. The soul is not defense enough against spiritual things. Your spirit, empowered by the Holy Spirit, is the defense you need to confront spiritual things that come up against you. There are soulish and diabolical prayers sent up by real witches, warlocks, *blind witches* and evil human agents, but those soulish prayers get waylaid in the second heaven where the seat of Satan is and they get empowered spiritually with an evil anointing.

What is in the *second heaven*? As said, the seat of Satan is there. Spiritual wickedness is there.

For we wrestle not against flesh and blood, but against principalities, against powers, against the rulers of the darkness of this world, against spiritual wickedness in high places. (Ephesians 6:12)

111

So the *spirits* that get attached to soulish prayers and empower them to come to pass, are demonic. Those evil incantations and enchantments are empowered by the powers of darkness. So, even soulish and diabolical "prayers" get a spiritual evil anointing. Just like curses, hexes, vexes, et cetera get powered up, demonically and then cannot be fended off by your soul, alone. Additionally, if Time is put on these evil covenants and the victim is unaware, this is how humans lose in the realms of spiritual warfare.

The Great Insult

It is the greatest insult to give someone your back, as they say. When you are pulled backward and you about-face, you give the vision for your life, you give your destiny, you give God your back.

Are you serious right now? Giving God your back? This is a serious test of Mercy if God is still the Lord of our lives and we give Him our back, and get duped into doing this over and over.

You didn't intend to or mean to insult God, did you? Insulting anyone is not a good way to get them to bless you.

You see another devil tactic here, how he gets man to do things to get him into trouble with God.

Prayers to Break Soul Ties

1. **Repent.** Repent for everything you can think to repent of. Repent every day. Repent of ever having formed a soul tie. Ask the Lord to break all deception off of your life and thinking, in the Name of Jesus.
2. **If you are soul tied because you believe the person hurt you, then forgive the person.** Release all unforgiveness, resentment and bitterness.
3. If you are soul-tied because you believe you love the other person and can't live without them, keep loving them, but turn it into *agape* love, wishing the best for them and what God has for their life.

Pray for hope and divine intervention that God will show you the purpose and the people who are to be in your life, and begin to do your purpose, reaching toward your own destiny. Ask the Lord to heal your heart and restore your soul.

4. If you are soul-tied and believe you can't live without them and they are coming back to you.

Ask the Lord as in #3 and also for a reality check. Maybe God needs to do a wellness check on your soul, because it may be scattered all over town or all over the world, depending on where the location where the soul tie took place.

Some say that soul ties don't exist, others say they do. Obsessions, crushes, being stuck – by any other name may describe a soul tie. If any part of your soul has crashed or is so busy that it is unavailable for daily chores and activities, then if it is not tied, then it is tied up. Like a computer message:
Server is busy, this file cannot be processed at this time.

Ungodly connections and entanglements create serious problems. It is bad enough when it is human to human, but when it is human to other, it seems we're asking for trouble because we are treading out into territory that we know nothing about. Further, how do we get back?

Attachment disorders? If you are attached or soul tied to someone who is disordered or is likely to be, then this will affect you adversely. *What is he doing? What is she doing?* Let's say this person is a party hound or a drug abuser; if you're soul tied to them and stalking them, where do you think you will find yourself?

Why do you have to break ungodly soul ties? Because they are ungodly, first of all, and because they can tie or yoke you to all kinds of *stuff* that you may not have yet discovered.

We came into the world alone and we will return and answer to God alone.

Tied to whom?

No one. This is mandatory.

A five-year-old wanted to know of his mom and dad, *How come you two get to sleep together, but I have to sleep by myself?*

Wow, kid. Yet, this is reality; we have so many things that we must do alone. Even if you marry, even if you check out of Earth on the same day as your spouse or anyone else, we all must give account for our own lives and our own souls, alone.

OK, team up and complete your projects you may hear in school. That's hard enough and it's one project. Marriage is hard because it is two folks trying to work in tandem and get things done. But to not be married but tied together--, to not even desire to be married but tied together--, *oh pls*. To be soul tied to someone that you don't even love and possibly hate, such as a person who hurt, attacked or offended you--, that's hell. .

The crux of this matter of soul ties is that a soul tie is created by an evil covenant. The evil covenant sponsors the soul tie. The evil covenant was made when a sin took place. Chances are, the person you sinned with is in the covenant with you. If two agree as touching---, what did you all *touch*? The unclean thing? The taboo thing? Whatever it was, you sinned, if you are perpetually tied to and in company of the person you sinned with, when will you break free from the sin and the iniquity of it?

Your **ride or die** needs to be saved, and *of God* and not of this world. Another human being may have tempted you to sin and they may always be a temptation for you to sin…, this person falls for the temptation to sin and drags you along with them. You're tied together, running buddies, stick buddies as they say.

Insisting on a soul tie tells God that you didn't do anything wrong. It tells God that you are not repenting and believe that you have no need to repent. It tells God you like the evil covenant and want to keep it. *This is not smart.*

The evil covenant? The curse? The iniquity? The demons that enforce the curse have a right to be in your life now--, *familiar spirits*, for example.

Prayers

From today, I unyoke myself from every satanic yoke and distance myself from every unrighteous relationship, in the Name of Jesus.

Lord, guide me to choose only Godly friends and relationships, in the Name of Jesus.

Father, disconnect me from all evil soul ties between myself and anyone that have been in any relationship with, whether sexual, emotional, familial, or otherwise, known or unknown, in the Name of Jesus.

Lord, forgive me of all sex sins, in the Name of Jesus; I repent.

Lord, forgive me for all wrong sex I've ever had, in the Name of Yeshua.

Lord, forgive me for anything that grieves or quenches the Holy Spirit in the Name of Yeshua.

Lord, forgive me for every unauthorized bed I've ever been in or even near, in the Name of Jesus.

Lord, remove the iniquity of Reuben which brought on the curse of: *thou shalt not excel,* in the Name of Yeshua.

Lord, as I encounter people, help me not to idolize them, in the Name of Jesus.

I break every evil covenant that allows a soul tie, in the Name of Jesus.

I renounce the sin that allowed the evil covenant, in the Name of Jesus.

I revoke the soul tie and break it and any yoke and bondage because of it, in the Name of Jesus.

Lord, reverse the damage that every soul tie has done to my life, in the Name of Jesus.

Lord, help me to set boundaries and establish Godly order in every relationship in my life, in the Name of Jesus.

Father, break the *people-pleasing spirit* off me, in the Name of Jesus.

Lord, in every moment of weakness, Holy Spirit wake me up from slumber and remind me who I am in Christ, in the Name of Jesus.

Curses hiding to fight me, blood of Jesus, expose and destroy them, in the Nname of Jesus.

Time-released curses, your time is up – **EXPIRE** against me, in the Name of Jesus.

Father, redeem me from harm and hurt and curses from the time that I didn't even know that witches were enchanting against me, in the Name of Yeshua.

Reverse all damages and restore to me all that has been lost, stolen, hidden and sequestered away from me, in the Name of Yeshua.

Lord, let my prayers and decrees go back and forth in time, in every dimension and realm to destroy the works of the devil, destroy the works of witchcraft against me.

I shut down every evil power working against me, my life, my destiny, my ministry, my career, my health, my finances, my kindom marriage, my kingdom children, my peace, love, and joy and abundance, in the Name of Jesus.

Curses & Time

There are other ways that Time is incorporated into curses that may be sent into a person's life and that is by triangulation with celestial powers and earthly elements. While this is different than being soul tied to a time or a time period from your past, it is of value to take a look at how curses can cause repetitive events in a person's life.

More on this can be gleaned from my book series on the Triangular Powers: *Powers Above* which includes **Sunblock, Don't Swear by the Moon**, and **Starstruck**

Your Own Words

Don't neglect the effect of your own words and how time can be incorporated into word curses that you, yourself have spoken over yourself or others. Saying things such as, *Every* holiday turns out like this. *Every* birthday it rains. *Every* month, this that or the other happens. *Every* time of the month I feel thus and so. *Every* time I meet someone new. Notice how time is built into your words and you can make problems cyclical in your life.

Using time-laced words and phrases such as *always, forever, ever and ever, to infinity* also bring Time into vows, oaths, and declarations.

Why not use those words to make **blessings** repetitive in your life?

- I am breaking every soul tie and closing every door that I may have opened to you through my unforgiveness and stupid wishful thinking, in the Name of Jesus.
- I break every soul tie between myself and any pastor, any political leader, or other authority figure, in the Name of Jesus.

Adam & Eve made a **covenant** with the Serpent and then before they could reach for the Tree of Live and add TIME, that is, **forever** onto it, God scurried them out of the Garden.

It's as simple as when you dip into the party dip, bite the chip, you don't bring that same chip you've bitten off back into the dip. That is called double dipping. It is nasty in the natural because your saliva is all over the bitten chip. God doesn't allow it in the spiritual because the Serpent's saliva, venom, and DNA is all over the evil contract that you made with him. While the devil can't then make a covenant with God, we can. So he tries to make a covenant with you and then get *you* to bring God into covenant.

It ain't happening. It's why folks who are already in a covenant with the devil, and devils can't get into Heaven, or may I say, *back* into Heaven.

Know ye not that the unrighteous shall not inherit the kingdom of God? Be not deceived: neither fornicators, nor idolaters, nor adulterers, nor effeminate, nor abusers of themselves with mankind,

Nor thieves, nor covetous, nor drunkards, nor revilers, nor extortioners, shall inherit the kingdom of God.

And such were some of you: but ye are washed, but ye are sanctified, but ye are justified in the name of the Lord Jesus, and by the Spirit of our God.
(1 Corinthians 6:9-11)

This verse doesn't mean you can't get saved and give up all these sins, that is, give up and renounce all evil covenants you have with the devil and now repent and turn and serve God. But it means that you must repent and renounce previous evil covenants in order to be saved and serve the Lord. When we get saved we get the authority to become sons of God. It is a process, an ongoing process; each day we choose in which direction we will go, whom we will serve. We must renounce evil devil contracts and not keep entering into new evil covenants--, even in error, or by mistake. The devil loves to trap man, that is why we must be wiser than he is so we do not get trapped or initiated into evil covenants, even *in* our salvation.

The sun, moon, stars, all the elements were made by God and belong to God, but evil agents misappropriate them for evil all the time. It is why we must command them and counter-command them. Got also made Time but it is misappropriated by the enemy as well--, it is one of the ways he traps mankind. Therefore, we must command Time and also counter-command it if it has been employed against us. Remember Time when dealing with covenants, contracts and even evil soul ties.

But I'm only soul-tied to a family member; what's wrong with that, you may argue? Don't argue with me, talk to God, prove what you believe in the Word of God.

If you are not appropriately in a relationship the way God says it should be, then you could be soul tied and cleaving more to the person than to God. Again, that's a form of idolatry and God hates idolatry.

He that loveth father or mother more than me is not worthy of me: and he that loveth son or daughter more than me is not worthy of me.

And he that taketh not his cross, and followeth after me, is not worthy of me.
(Matthew 10:37-38)

Even being soul tied to someone because you believe you love them is still evil. It is evil because the devil is in the soul tie. It can be evil because it means you have venerated the object of your soul tie too much; you have idolized them.

If the two of you have broken up, it's as though you have memorialized them in yesterday, how they *used* to be, what they used to look like, how they used to treat you. You've made them into a statue really and now you worship the statue. I say statue because you've frozen them in time, in your mind. They've moved on, but you are still in yesterday.

When you play or hear your song, for example, the song you used to share together, listen to together, or dance to together, you *bow*. Daniel wouldn't and God gave us that lesson so we wouldn't also. You may feel that no evil power is making you bow when the music is played. It is subtle, but you are being made to bow. Even if you lower your head and weep just a little because you miss them, you are bowing. Even if you lower your head because you are sad, you are bowing. Even if you don't really genuflect or bow, you are approaching the virtual statue that you made in your mind and observing it, and to a demon or a devil, that is worship.

And looking back, you've turned yourself into a pillar of salt.

Finally, brethren, whatsoever things are true, whatsoever things are honest, whatsoever things are just, whatsoever things are pure, whatsoever things are lovely, whatsoever things are of good report; if there be any virtue, and if there be any praise, think on these things. (Philippians 4:8)

Dear Reader

Thank you for acquiring, reading, and sharing this book. When the Past is calling, don't answer.

Ask the Lord for Wisdom because if you are soul tied to a not-so-nice person, they may like having that power over you, even though they have no intention of getting back together with you. I pray the Lord will empower you to break every evil covenant and every evil soul tie,

In the Name of Jesus,

Amen.

Dr. Marlene Miles

Prayer books by this author

While most books by this author have prayer points either throughout the book or at the end, there are some books that are **only** prayers. You just open up the book and pray. They are listed below:

Prayers Against Barrenness: *For Success in Business and Life*

Fruit of the Womb: *Prayers Against Barrenness*

Beauty Curses, *Warfare Prayers Against*
https://a.co/d/5Xlc20M

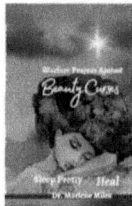

Courts of Marriage: Prayers for Marriage in the Courts of Heaven
(prayerbook) https://a.co/d/cNAdgAq

Courtroom Warfare @ Midnight
(prayerbook) https://a.co/d/5fc7Qdp

Demonic Cobwebs *(prayerbook)*
https://a.co/d/fp9Oa2H

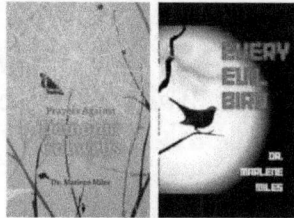

Every Evil Bird https://a.co/d/hF1kh1O

Every Evil Arrow
https://a.co/d/afgRkiA

Gates of Thanksgiving

Spirits of Death & the Grave, Pass Over Me and My House
https://a.co/d/dS4ewyr

Please note that my name is spelled incorrectly on amazon, but not on the book.

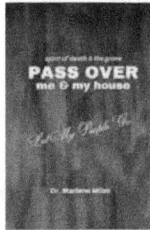

Throne of Grace: Courtroom Prayer

https://a.co/d/fNMxcM9

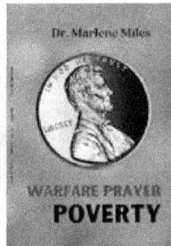

Warfare Prayer Against Poverty
https://a.co/d/bZ611Yu

Other books by this author

AK: *The Adventures of the Agape Kid*

AMONG SOME THIEVES

Ancestral Powers https://a.co/d/9prTyFf

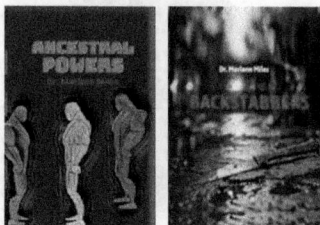

Backstabbers https://a.co/d/gi8iBxf

Barrenness, *Prayers Against*
https://a.co/d/feUltIs

Battlefield of Marriage, *The*

Blindsided: *Has the Old Man
Bewitched You?* https://a.co/d/5O2fLLR

Break Free from Collective Captivity

Casting Down Imaginations
https://a.co/d/1UxlLqa

Churchcraft: Witchcraft In the Church

Churchzilla, The Wanna-Be, Supposed-to-be Bride of Christ

Curses of Blind Men

Demonic Cobwebs (prayerbook)

Demonic Time Bombs

Demons Hate Questions

Devil Loves Trauma, *The*

Devil Weapons: Unforgiveness, Bitterness,...

The Devourers: *Thieves of Darkness 2*

Do Not Swear by the Moon

Don't Refuse Me, Lord (4 book series)

https://a.co/d/idP34LG

Dream Defilement

The Emptiers: *Thieves of Darkness, 1*
https://a.co/d/5I4n5mc

Every Evil Arrow
https://a.co/d/afgRkiA

Evil Touch https://a.co/d/gSGGpS1

Failed Assignment
https://a.co/d/3CXtjZY

Fantasy Spirit Spouse
https://a.co/d/hW7oYbX

FAT Demons (The): *Breaking Demonic Curses*

The Fold (5-book series)

- The Fold (Book 1)
- Name Your Seed (Book 2)
- The Poor Attitudes of Money (3)
- Do Not Orphan Your Seed (4)
- For the Sake of the Gospel (5)
- My Sowing Journal

Gang Ups: *Touch Not God's Anointed*

got HEALING? Verses for Life

got LOVE? Verses for Life

got HOPE? Verses for Life

got money? https://a.co/d/g2av41N

How to Dental Assist

How to Dental Assist2: Be Productive, Not Wasteful

I Take It Back

Legacy

Let Me Have A Dollar's Worth
https://a.co/d/h8F8XgE

Level the Playing Field

Living for the NOW of God

Lose My Location
https://a.co/d/crD6mV9

Man Safari, *The*

Marriage Ed. Rules of Engagement & Marriage

Made Perfect in Love

Money Hunters: Beware of Those

Money on the Altar https://a.co/d/4EqJ2Nr

Mulberry Tree https://a.co/d/9nR9rRb

Motherboard (The) - *Soul Prosperity Series*

Name Your Seed

Occupy: *Until I Return*

Plantation Souls

Players Gonna Play

Power Money: Nine Times the Tithe
https://a.co/d/gRt41gy

The Power of Wealth *(forthcoming)*

Powers Above

Remember the Time https://a.co/d/3PbBjkF

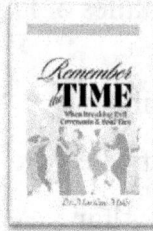

Repent of Visiting Evil Altars
https://a.co/d/3n3Zjwx

The Robe, *Part 1, The Lessons of Joseph*

The Robe, *The Lessons of Joseph* Part II,

Seasons of Grief

Seasons of Waiting

Seasons of War

Second Marriage, Third--, *Any Marriage*

https://a.co/d/6m6GN4N

Seducing Spirits: *Idolatry & Whoredoms*

Sift You Like Wheat

Six Men Short: What Has Happened to all the Men?

Soul Prosperity, Soul Prosperity Series Book 3 https://a.co/d/5p8YvCN

Soulish & Diabolical Prayer Treatment

Souls In Captivity, Soul Prosperity Series Book 2

The Spirit of Poverty

StarStruck

SUNBLOCK

The Swallowers: *Thieves of Darkness*, Book 3

Take It Back

This Is NOT That: How to Keep Demons from Coming at You

Time Is of the Essence

Too Many Wives: *Why You Have Lady Problems*

Tormenting Spirits https://a.co/d/dAogEJf

Toxic Souls

Triangular Power *(series)*

- Powers Above
- SUNBLOCK
- Do Not Swear by the Moon
- STARSTRUCK

Uncontested Doom

Unguarded Hours, *The*

Unseen Life, *The* https://a.co/d/0drZ5Ll

Upgrade: How to Get Out of Survival Mode

- Toxic Souls (Book 2 of series)

- Legacy (Book 3 of series)

The Wasters: *Thieves of Darkness*, Bk 2
https://a.co/d/bUvI9Jo

What Have You to Declare? What Do You Have With You from Where You've Been?

When I Was A Child, *I Prayed As a Child*

When the Devourer is Rebuked

https://a.co/d/1HVv8oq

The Wilderness Romance *(series)* This series is about conducting a Godly relationship and marriage with someone who is a Wilderness person. It is about how to recognize it and navigate through it. These books are about how not to get caught up in such.

- *The Social Wilderness*
- *The Sexual Wilderness*
- *The Spiritual Wilderness*

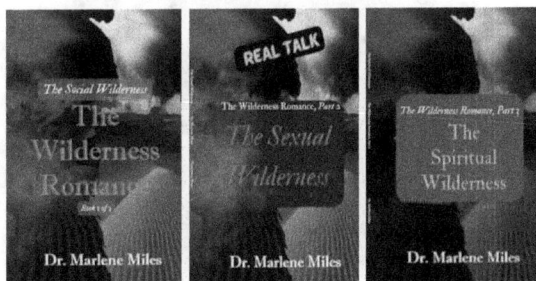

Other Series

The Fold (a series on Godly finances)
https://a.co/d/4hz3unj

Soul Prosperity Series https://a.co/d/bz2M42q

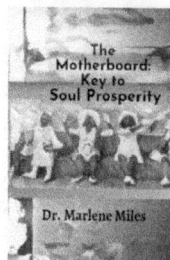

Spirit Spouse books

https://a.co/d/9VehDSo

https://a.co/d/97sKOwm

Thieves of Darkness series

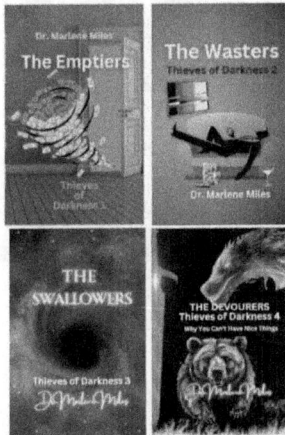

Triangular Powers https://a.co/d/aUCjAWC

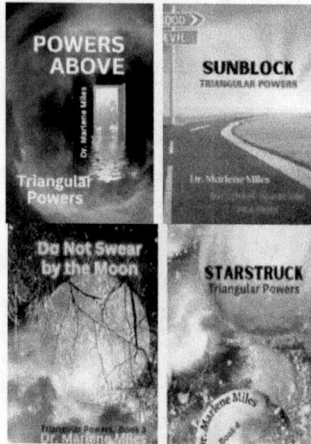

Upgrade (series) *How to Get Out of Survival Mode* https://a.co/d/aTERhX0

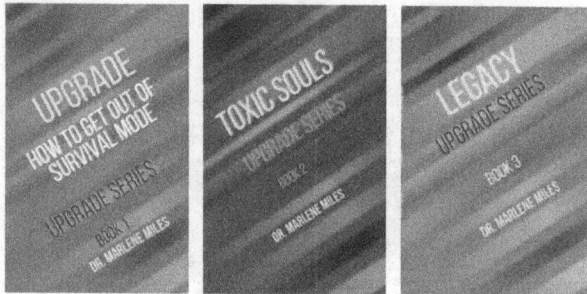

www.ingramcontent.com/pod-product-compliance
Lightning Source LLC
LaVergne TN
LVHW052029080426
835513LV00018B/2240